Love - Kingdom Vibes Only

Tanique Somers

Scripture quotations marked AMP are from The Holy Bible: The Amplified Bible. 1987. 2015. La Habra, CA: The Lockman Foundation

Scripture quotations marked TPT are from The Passion Translation®. Copyright © 2017, 2018, 2020 by Passion & Fire Ministries, Inc. Used by permission. All rights reserved. ThePassionTranslation.com.

Design by: Ryan Kerbs
Published by: Tanique Somers
Printed in the United States of America

ISBN 979-8-9868450-0-5

Dedication

This is dedicated to everyone who is on the journey of discovering the height, depth, and breadth of God's love and how to be a vessel and channel of it.

Acknowledgments

A big thanks to my family and friends who have been along for this crazy ride. Thanks to my My Generation Church family for believing in me and supporting my dream wholeheartedly. Thank you to all who purchased my first spur of the moment poetry collection, "The Mischief of Love", it gave me the confidence to do this book. A big shout out to Ryan Kerb Design for my book cover design and page layout. Shout out to you, holding this book!!

Description

Love-Kingdom Vibes Only, is a unique Christian poetry collection that includes prayer challenges, journal prompts, activities and devotionals for you to engage with as you read.

It is separated into five sections, which illustrate different modes of love. The reader will traverse the ups and downs of self-love, romantic love, familial love, communal love, and "Divine" love- which is loving our Creator God.

As you read and interact with the activities, you will have an opportunity to self-reflect and see what the bible has to say about love and our relationships. It is my hope that you will be able to incorporate God's principles into your relationships as you read his Word and it transforms your heart. May your love to all, be kingdom vibes only!

Table of Contents

Foreword

"So above all, constantly seek God's kingdom and his righteousness, then all these less important things will be given abundantly." Matthew 6:33 TPT

What is the greatest thing we all desperately search for and many deem it impossible to live without? Love. Yet, the bible counts it has less important. This verse was given a new meaning after reading, The Sacred Search by Gary Thomas. He illustrates that we should "seek God's kingdom and righteousness" and we should also do so in our relationships. Often times we associate the idea of seeking righteousness as morality and love and relationships are more subjective in nature.

This is where the inspiration from Jerry Flowers Jr.'s sermon series "#Kingdomvibesonly came in. His intent was to push his congregants to think heavenward. It is my hope that as you read these poems and engage with the suggested activities, that you will be able to see God's kingdom principles when it comes to love, as it relates to self love, romantic love, familiar love, love in community, and loving God. I pray that this book will serve as a reminder that your love for self and others should look more and more like God's love for us every day.

This book is a reflection of my own love journey. I had to arrive at a place where I embraced the reality of my past and extend grace to my inner child. The healing that is produced I believe will open the path to deeper intimacy with God. In this way, I would be better equipped to bring glory to God in all my relationships, especially my partnership with my future spouse to create safety in our union which will produce children who are equipped to take part in the cosmic battle. If we uphold the kingdom principles in our home, consequently our influence will diffuse into our communities by the way we treat each other. We would be evidence that God exists! The existence of Love is the proof that God exists. God is love!

We have learned overtime that love is transactional, fair and conditional. Through this journey, I have learned that love is not fair, not always about receiving, never ending and it is not self-centered. Love is other (outward) facing. But in order for us to get to this awareness, it may require healing and most definitely require understanding our identity in Christ. In the New Testament times, they had the luxury of having multiple words for love unlike the English-speaking readers. God calls us to exercise all of them for his glory, not solely for our gratification. God defines himself by using the word love and he defines his kingdom as not solely a physical place, but a place found within us where his presence dwells. So as the title suggests, it is my sincere hope that this book sets you on a path to engender love that could only be inspired by God's heavenly Kingdom found in you through the work of the Holy Spirit. Selah!

With Love, To Me

In the Kingdom: There is
acceptance and restoration.

The Temple

Your body is a treasure,

That's why it attracted so many pirates.

But this doesn't mean...that though

   it may have been desecrated

That God can't restore it to its original grandeur.

"Have you forgotten that your body is now the sacred temple of the Spirit of Holiness, who lives in you? You don't belong to yourself any longer, for the gift of God, the Holy Spirit lives inside your sanctuary."

1 Corinthians 6:19 TPT

Beauty

You are different,

And that's where your beauty lies.

Beauty is you.

"Let your true beauty come from your inner personality, not a focus on the external. For lasting beauty comes from a gentle and peaceful spirit which is precious in God's sight and is much more important than the outward adornment of elaborate hair, jewelry and fine clothes."

1 Peter 3:3-4 TPT

Prayer Challenge #1

Journal

Take a moment and make a list of all the

intrinsic qualities you love about yourself.

Pray

- Thank God for making you unique
- Ask him to help you embrace and show up more and more the way he has created you to be.

Friends

Books are great teachers but not
   God's idea for friends.

"The man of too many friends [chosen indiscrimi-
nately] will be broken in pieces and come to ruin,
but there is a [true, loving] friend who [is reliable
and] sticks closer than a brother."

Proverbs 18:24 AMP

Silence

Silence is not always golden.
I wish our silence didn't make so
    many people comfortable.

"If the Lord had not been my help, I would soon
have dwelt in the land of silence."

Psalms 94:17 AMP

Polyglot

Maybe you learned new languages because
you were trying to find your voice.

"I poured out my complaint to you, God. I lifted up
my voice, shouting out for your help."

Psalms 77:1 TPT

Advocate

You became the voice for the voiceless

    because you knew what it was like

    when pain pushed the mute button.

"And in a similar way, the Holy Spirit takes hold of us in our human frailty to empower us in our weakness. For example, at times we don't even know how to pray or know the best things to ask for. But the Holy Spirit rises up within us to super-intercede on our behalf, pleading to God with emotional sighs too deep for words."

Romans 8:26 TPT

Meditation #1

I love that, in many ways in scripture, God is willing to show up as our advocate and defender. Sometimes our circumstances force us into silence not because it doesn't hurt but because of who it may hurt if we do speak up.

Often times, we feel like our cases will never be heard. That justice will never be served. But I encourage you to do what David did and cry out to God, day and night about the injustices, anxieties, literally everything. I can assure you that God sees and cares. He is Jehovah Tsaba, he will fight for you.

Read:

- Psalms 35

Acclimate

You have an uncanny capability of

adapting to bad situations, let's

learn to embrace the good.

"So we are convinced that every detail of our
lives is continually woven together for good, for
we are his lovers who have been called to fulfill
his designed purpose."

Romans 8:28 TPT

Detached

Don't confuse numbness for strength.

"But he answered me, "My grace is always more than enough for you, and my power finds its full expression through your weaknesses." So I will celebrate my weaknesses, for when I'm weak I sense more deeply the mighty power of Christ living in me."

2 Corinthians 12:9 TPT

Auditions

Brokenness turns your life into a constant
    casting call for a play you didn't even write
Every relationship becomes an audition

Wholeness reminds you that you are
    the casting director and producer
Recasting roles is your honor and duty
The role is yours

"A friend loves at all times, And a brother is born
for adversity."

Proverbs 17:17 AMP

Vice

Don't confuse productivity as

    being purpose driven,

  it was simply a safe drug.

"Give God the right to direct your life, and as you trust him along the way, you'll find he pulled it off perfectly!"

Psalms 37:5 TPT

Lotus flower

Some of the world's most beautiful things were

born in the ugliest places and circumstances.

"...I feel as dark and dry as the desert tents of
the wandering nomads. Yet you are so lovely—
like the fine linen tapestry hanging in the Holy
Place."

Song of Songs 1:5 TPT

The other 50

The divorce was not your fault.

You were not the irreconcilable difference.

Unfortunately, they still accomplished

   splitting you 50-50.

"...But you have received the "Spirit of full accep-
tance," enfolding you into the family of God. And
you will never feel orphaned, for as he rises up
within us, our spirits join him in saying the words
of tender affection, "Beloved Father!" For the
Holy Spirit makes God's fatherhood real to us as
he whispers into our innermost being, " You are
God's beloved child!"

Romans 8:15-16 TPT

Love-Kingdom Vibes Only

Parent's Day

There are days when your life

    giver may smother the life they

    gave you with their words.

There will come a day,

When you will need to unlearn the lessons

    taught by their wounded hearts.

Your wounded inner child will need to

    grow up into a healed mother.

You will speak life.

Reclaiming your original identity as Eve.

And you just may need to become the mother

    to your mother that you always needed.

Maybe honoring your parents is understanding

    and accepting that there may be

    inadequacies and disappointments ahead,

"But love covers a multitude of sin."

Honor is to see them as humans

And to respect that God chose them.

Parents are humans not superheroes.

And his mercy is upon generation after gener-
ation toward those who [stand in great awe of
God and] fear Him.

Luke 1:50 AMP

The unlearning

Learning about what not to do is still

    a crucial part of learning.

"And if anyone longs to be wise, ask God for wisdom and he will give it! He won't seek your lack of wisdom as an opportunity to scold you over your failures but he will overwhelm your failures with his generour grace."

James 1:5 TPT

Footsteps

Somehow you don't remember when

    your parents left, that's because those

    were the moments God stepped in

    and fulfilled his promises to you.

"When your mother and father [abandons]

    you that he will [adopt] you." *

He never dropped you.

That's why you don't remember

    hitting the ground.

"My father and mother abandoned me. But you, Yahweh, took me in and made me yours."

Psalms 27:10 TPT*

"To the fatherless he is a father. To the widow he is a champion friend. The lonely he makes part of a family. The prisoners [bitter ones] he leads into prosperity until they sing for joy."

Psalms 68:5-6 TPT

Dauntless

The best thing about you is that you still
dauntlessly believe. The best thing about
you is that you dauntlessly still believe.

"Jesus was astonished when he heard this and
said to those who were following him, "He has
greater faith than anyone I've encountered in
Israel!"

Matthew 8:10 TPT

Congratulations

Congratulations on all your report cards,

    even the C's because even when you

    were not at your best you kept trying.

"Then suddenly the voice of the Father shouted from the sky saying, "This is my Son-the Be-loved! My greatest delight is in him."

Matthew 3:17 TPT

Perfect

I am made whole

I am perfected in God's love

He dances over me with singing

You, therefore will be perfect [growing into
spiritual maturity both in mind and character,
actively integrating godly values into your daily
life], as your heavenly Father is perfect.

Matthew 5:48 AMP

Shine

My body is God's dwelling place

He shines from within

So I will not look at it with contempt

But make the necessary adjustments

For his glory to shine through

You were bought with a price [you were actually purchased with the precious blood of Jesus and made his own]. So then, honor and glorify God with your body.

1 Corinthians 6:20 AMP

Invitation

My flaws are just invitations

For God's hands to mold me

But the vessel that he was making from clay
was spoiled by the potter's hand; so he made it
over, reworking it and making it into another pot
that seemed good to him. Then the word of the
Lord came to me: "O house of Israel, can I not
do with you as this potter does? says the Lord."
Look carefully, as the clay is in the potter's hand,
so are you in my hand, O house of Israel.

Jeremiah 18:4–6 AMP

Love-Kingdom Vibes Only

Prayer Challenge #2:

Talk to God about any trauma you experienced (physically, emotionally, and sexually).

- Ask God to restore your body, soul and mind to its original grandeur.
- Ask him to help you experience the love of the Father through the comfort of the Holy Spirit.
- Ask God to give you the courage and strength to forgive and release those who may have hurt you knowingly or unknowingly

Kingdom Romance

In the Kingdom: There is safety
and sacrifice in intimacy.

Power Couple

"Strength is made perfect in weakness"
So I lay this lifeless body down on the altar
Daily dying
So He could be strong in me for us

No one ever said that when I
    walked down that aisle
It would be my last day living
Last day living for me
Now I'm speaking French
Oui, we
Yes, we
Yes, us
Yes, I do

I never knew the beauty that could
    come in walking with a limp
I asked Him to take it away
But instead He sent me you
"It felt good to find someone worthy of needing"
Neyo said,
"You're the best thing I never knew I needed."

I attended your funeral everyday
In that realm
I saw you
A purple robe draped your body
As martyrs
Your ego and will
Surrendered their last breaths
You gave your life over to your King

Prostrate
You waited for instructions from
    your Commander in Chief
You thought it not robbery
To give away all you had
For the greatest love of all is a
    love that sacrifices all.
And this great love is demonstrated when
    a man sacrifices his life for his family.
I love the way you die

As living sacrifices
Hand in hand
Let us daily cast ourselves onto the mercy seat
And the gates of Sheol will not
    prevail against us
Power couple

"This is how we have discovered love's reali-
ty: Jesus sacrificed his life for us. Because of his
great love, we should be willing to lay down our
lives for one another.

1 John 3:16 TPT

"Be free from pride-filled opinions, for they
will only harm your cherished unity. Don't allow
self-promotion to hide in your hearts, but in au-
thentic humility put others first and view others
as more important than yourselves. Abandon
every display of selfishness. Possess a greater
concern for what matters to others instead of
your own interests. And consider the example
that Jesus, the Anointed One, has set before us.
Let his mindset become your motivation."

Philippians 2:3–5 TPT

Meditation #2

I've often wondered why God chose marriage to emulate his relationship with us. In our world, everything including marriage must serve the purpose of fulfilling our needs and if it doesn't "on to the next one."

In the context of the way God illustrated his love for us through his Son, it was not how well we could serve him but how much he sacrificed/offered for us, and he made sure to sacrifice his best.

Myrrh is a symbol of suffering which was offered to Mary and Joseph foreshadowing the suffering that Jesus' love gift to us would be mingled with pain.(Fentress et al.) We also see this prophetically in Song of Songs 5. Often times when we recite those sacred vows at the altar, we secretly hope that the "or for worse" never comes. But how does one prove genuinity if not by the fire. We are reminded in scripture that we will not take part in the heavenly celebration if we do not join in the suffering of Christ (Philippians 3:10 AMP).

Marriage is the perfect school to become more like God. It requires a constant laying down/mortification of self and seeking the best outcome for the other person.

There is also a temptation to neglect this truth because of the "bad rep" marriage gets but there is supposed to be delight and bliss in marriage (not just in the "honeymoon phase") as well. Similarly, God also wants us to delight in his presence. This is another reason I believe God uses marriage to symbolize his relationship with us.

Lastly, it's not enough to know of your partner in marriage, you should have, as the original meaning of the word suggests ,an experiential knowledge of your person.There should be an emotionally safe space to know your partner in ways that are unique to you.

This goes without saying but God created us to be able to walk and talk with him freely as he did with Adam. He enjoyed our company. He did all he did for our salvation to restore the opportunity to be intimate with us again. It is our job to choose daily to meet with him in the gardens of our hearts.

Read:
- Song of Songs 5:1-2
- Matthew 2:11
- Psalms 37:4
- Psalms 18:19
- Psalms 27:4
- Philippians 3:10

Prayer Challenge #5

- Pray that God gives you the strength and endurance to weather the storms of life with your significant other, friends,and God.

- Ask God to help you to glorify his kingdom with your (future) marriage (and with your lives.)

- Ask God to help you identify ways you could improve your intimacy with Him

- Ask God to help you to identify the blockers of intimacy with God and people

You University

Hello
I would like to be admitted to the You university
I want to master the insatiable degree
    of knowledge that is found in the
    topography of your mind and soul
Let me fill my schedule with a little archeology
    to plumb the depths of your wisdom
Allow me to run experiments in the
    organic chemistry lab of your heart
For from it flows biology

Let's take a moment to review the syllabus
"Be fruitful and multiply"
Divide Algebra Calculus
Calculating if you and I can equal 1
Excuse me sir, Is there a seat available?

I would like to be enrolled in You university?
No, I wouldn't like to audit the class
But I am looking for an independent study
Something like a doctoral program

I'm here to bind up!
I'm here to transplant!
I'm here to resurrect!

I'm here to be a lifelong learner
If you're willing to be my Professor

"Now the Lord God said, It is not good (benefi-
cial) for the man to be alone; I will make him a
helper [one who balances him- a counterpart
who is] suitable and complementary for him."

Genesis 2:18 AMP

Gift

They say life is a gift

Tell me what's the purpose of a gift not shared?

Can a gift box not be ripped open?

What's the purpose of a gift not discovered?

What's the purpose of a gift not multiplied?

Can a true gift be given without

    the risk of rejection?

They say, "Life's deepest meaning is not found

    in accomplishments but in relationships."

Tell me, will you accept this gift?

"And the rib which the Lord God had taken from
the man He made (fashioned, formed) into a
woman, and He brought her and presented her
to the man."

Genesis 2:22 AMP

For one

I've heard it all
But I'm waiting for the words from mine.
For the one who saw me as an asset
Made a long term investment
And kept on giving .

It's one thing to be visible
But I'm waiting to be seen by one.
For his God given X-ray eyes
To parse through truths said and unsaid.
To hear on the frequency of my heart
Yeah it beats for one.

My Dear beloved
To be known
To be seen
To be heard
By you
Is all my heart has ever wanted!

"The Shulamite Woman: I am truly his rose, the
very theme of his song. I'm overshadowed by his
love, like a lily growing in the valley!

The Shepherd-King Yes, you are my darling
companion. You stand out from all the rest. For
though the thorns surround you, you remain
pure as lily, more than all others."

Song of Songs 2:1–2 TPT

Meditation #5

"The Shulamite Woman:I am truly his rose, the very theme of his song. I'm overshadowed by his love, like a lily growing in the valley!

The Shepherd-King Yes, you are my darling companion. You stand out from all the rest. For though the thorns surround you, you remain pure as lily, more than all others."

Song of Songs 2:1-2 TPT

Many of us have gone through trials and traumas but not many of us can say we came out unscathed and that's ok. That is not the real flex. I like that the text exalted purity of heart and not beauty, because purity is intrinsic. These "thorns" as the text calls them often may change our perspective or other external things.

However when it gets harmful is when as a protective measure its seeps into our characters and changes our identity. It isn't easy to go through these circumstances and remain pure in heart, but guess what? God notices. "For he doesn't look at the outward appearance, he looks at the heart"

1 Samuel 16:7.

Another point, I saved until now is this. "I'm over-shadowed by his love, like a lily growing in the valley!" It can seem like we are in a low place, but what makes a valley, being surrounded by mountains! This text means that his love that is as big as mountains covers you even if you feel as small as a lily in comparison.

We also should consider the size of the mountains, the lily is being protected. I want to point out the fact that these particular lilies are common and grow wild, yet he noticed this lily above the rest and this is to remind you that he sees you.

In those moments when you are down in the valley, look up and know that you are surrounded by love and protection as big and wide as the mountains!Love covers and protects.

Read:

- 1 Chronicles 16:11
- Psalms 88:2
- Psalms 32:7
- Deuteronomy 31:8

Lighthouse

When my words can stand

    before you undressed

And my thoughts finish first

    place in the Indie 500

And my heart beats at Mach 3

And you're summoned by my furrowed brow

Standing strong and still

In my emotional Hurricane

I'll know

My Lighthouse is on the horizon

"This hope [this confident assurance] we have as an anchor of the soul [it cannot slip and it cannot break down under whatever pressure bears upon it]—a safe and steadfast hope that enter within the veil [of the heavenly temple, that most Holy Place in the very presence of God dwells],"

Hebrews 6:19 AMP

Vacation

I want us to be each other's vacation.

May our words be as light as the breeze

And our kisses hot like the sun.

May our arms be like the waves

    which engulfs us.

As the moon is to the waves may our

    attraction for each other never die.

May the reasons for our love be

    as numerous as the sand.

May our eyes twinkle bright as the nights

    sky at the sight of our reflection.

May the buffet of our love be all we can eat.

May we only swim in the infinity

    pool of joy and peace.

May the view of eternity together

    inspire generations.

May our time together escape time itself.

Let's be each other's vacation.

"Love is large and incredibly patient. Love is gentle and consistently kind to all. It refuses to be jealous...Love does not traffic in shame and disrespect, nor selfishly seek its own honor. Love is not easily irritated or quick to take offense. Love joyfully celebrates honesty...Love is a safe place of shelter, for it never stops believing the best for other others... Love never stops loving."

1 Corinthians 13:4-8 TPT

3.I am fully devoted to my beloved,and my beloved is fully devoted to me.

The Bridegroom-King

4 O my beloved, you are lovely.When I see you in your beauty,I see a radiant city where we will dwell as one. More pleasing than any pleasure, more delightful than any delight, you have ravished my heart,stealing away my strength to resist you.Even hosts of angels stand in awe of you.

Song of Songs 6:3-4 TPT

Cherish the day

I will cherish the day when our eyes lock for
    the first time and we exchange our first
    skipped heartbeat and missed breath.
I will cherish the day that the world stops
    as our worlds collide into a kiss.
I will cherish the day that I catch
    myself staring at you from across
    the room ...and getting caught.
I will cherish the moment our eyes
    brighten at the sight of each other.
I will cherish all those talks about everything.
I will cherish all those walks to nowhere.
I will cherish all those laughing sessions.
I will cherish every moment in your arms,
    by your side, in your prayers.
I will cherish that one time we thought
    we would lose each other.
I will cherish the day we say we're glad we didn't.
I cherish the day we said I do.

"Let him smother me with kisses- his Spirit-kiss
divine. So kind are your caresses, I drink them in
like the sweetest wine!"

Song of Songs 1:2 TPT

Have you ever?

Have you ever missed someone you never met?

Have you ever reminisced on the good

    times you will share together?

"...Where is he—my soul's true love? He is no-
where to be found!"

Song of Songs 3:2

8 count Bachata

I already know why I'll love you,

Your masculinity.

The way you remind me to let you lead

And how great you look leading.

The strength you exude in the way

   you protect me as you guide me

   across the dance floor of life.

The way you let me spin and add my own

   steps and even off beat ones while the

   sparkle in your eye never fades.

I'll love you because even when I step on your

   feet or get too overwhelmed by my missteps

You find a way to get us back on beat, patiently.

Step by step

8 counts

You keep me within arm's reach.

But there's nothing better than being 1 inch

   away and knowing no one else exists on

   the dance floor besides you and me.

You spin me

Reminding me to notice myself and my beauty.

You pull me in, slowing me down

Reminding me of healthy boundaries.

Then we mirror each other's steps

    reminding us that we are one and

    we should move in synchrony.

8 steps of an infinity number of

    steps left to take with you.

You take my hand firmly yet gently.

Your eyes ablaze warmed my very soul

That's how I know that I will dance on this

    dance floor of life with you forever.

This is for the best dance partner

    a girl could ever pray for.

"Arise, my darling! Come quickly, my beloved. Come and be the graceful gazelle with me. Come be like a young stag with me. We will dance in the high place of the sky, yes, on the mountains of fragrant spice. Forever we shall be united as one!

Song of Songs 8:14 TPT

Just so you know

Just so you know...
You are (were) worth the wait.
You are loved.
I respect you.
You are intelligent.
You are handsome /beautiful.
You will be very successful.
You are more than enough.
You are blessed.
You are forgiven.
You are an overcomer.
You are strong.
You are wise.
You are an amazing father/mother
and even better husband/wife.
You are trustworthy
You are a King/Queen.

Just in case you ever forget your identity
 this is your friendly reminder. I will
 never get tired of reminding you.

Just so you know...

"Then Adam said, "This is now bone of my bones
and flesh of my flesh. She shall be called Wom-
an. Because she was taken out of Man."

                              Gen 2:22 AMP

The man named his wife Eve (life spring,life giv-
er), because she was the mother of all the living.

                              Gen.3:20 AMP

Prayer Challenge #4:

- Pray about any generational habits you want to unlearn from your upbringing
- Pray about forgiving and releasing any pain, guilt and shame you have about your past
- Ask the Lord to help you be a better channel of love to your (future) spouse
- Ask the Lord to cultivate the fruits of the spirit in you
- Ask the Lord to help you to discern the qualities of a healthy romantic partner
- Ask the Lord to bring spiritual mentors into your life to create new positive habits, beliefs and behaviors

Ponder/Journal:

Who are your marital role models/mentors? What are your hopes/fears concerning marriage?

The Union

When you look at me do you see Divinity?

When you speak, speak with reverence

For this space we share is holy

He resides here

Man, woman, God, The Trinity

"For this reason a man is to leave his father and his mother and lovingly hold to his wife, since the two became joined as one flesh. Marriage is the beautiful design of the Almighty, a great mystery of Christ and his church. So every married man should be gracious to his wife just as he is gracious to himself. And every wife should be tenderly devoted to her husband."

Ephesians 5:31–33 TPT

"For this reason a man shall leave his father and his mother , and shall be joined to his wife; and they shall become one flesh."

Gen 2:24 AMP

I Don't Wanna

I don't wanna ever miss that gleam in your eye

Or the tenderness in your voice

I don't wanna live another lifetime uncovered

Uncovered by your anointing

Uncovered by your protection

I don't wanna miss the opportunity of serving

you honor on the platter of my submission

While we are subbing under the same mission

I don't wanna walk outside of your shadow

You are my sole mate.

I don't wanna go back to life without you.

No, I don't wanna.

"I know my lover is mine and I have everything in
you, for we delight ourselves in each other."

Song of Songs 2:16 TPT

Soft life

Can you be that soft place to lay my head,

when my mind is filled with dread?

Can I brace on you the weight of my soul,

when my hope has turned to coal?

Can you haul me on to the pick–

    up truck of your prayers,

when my words have caught a flat?

"Listen, my radiant one—if you ever lose sight of me, just follow in my footsteps where I lead my lovers. Come with your burdens and cares…"

Song of Songs 1: 8 TPT

"Are you weary, carrying a heavy burden? Come to me. I will refresh your life, for I am your oasis."

Matthew 11:28 TPT

Boxing ring

When you're done sparring in the ring called life,
I hope you will run back to the corner of
    the ring and find safety in my arms.
As I dress your wounds with the
    salve of affirmations
Tighten your gloves with prayer
May I never enter the ring as your opponent
But as your sparring partner
Ever ready to prepare you for the fight ahead
I pray you make it through all rounds
And that the corner will never be silent
Even at your lowest moment
Above all the noise
I'll make it be known
How proud I am to be in your corner!

"His massive arms are wrapped around you,
protecting you. You can run under his covering
of majesty and hide. His arms of faithfulness
are as a shield keeping you from harm."

Psalms 91:4 TPT

"Love is a safe place of shelter..."

1 Corinthians 13:7 TPT

Rest

In your love

I get to be off the clock

In peace [and with a tranquil heart] I will both lie down and sleep, For You alone, O lord, make me dwell in safety and confident trust.

Psalms 4:8 AMP

Prayer Challenge #5:

- Ask the Holy Spirit to help you to be a safe place for those around you
- Ask the Holy Spirit to reveal ways in which you have not been putting others first in your relationships
- Ask God to show you who needs more of your love today
- Ask God to help you to experience his love for you every day
- Ask God to give you the strength to let go of unhealthy relationships

Do:

How can you best serve your significant other, parent, friend, or child, today? (Expecting nothing in return). You can refer to the 5 Love Languages book/quiz by Gary Chapman.

- Give a compliment to your significant other, parent, friend, or child today
- Give your undivided attention to your significant other, parent, friend, child
- Give a just because gift to someone
- Do something on a loved ones to do list

Read

- 1 Corinthians 13
- Ephesians 5

Journal

- What is the mission/vision of your life/(future) marriage/family?

Kingdom Family

Love-Kingdom Vibes Only

In the Kingdom: There are
generational blessings.

Creation

I was created to be loved

So were you

In love we created them

Now love is set on replay

Because in the beginning there was love

God is love

Then we, your devoted lovers, will forever thank
you, praising your name from generation to
generation!

Psalms 79:13 TPT

Love—Kingdom Vibes Only

To my baby girl

My sweet one,

I believe you.

I believe you when you say you will be a dancing astronaut who bakes cookies on the moon.

And I will also believe you when you say

 That man made you feel scared.

I see you.

I hear you.

I will protect you.

Behold, children are a heritage and gift from the Lord, The fruit of the womb a reward.

Psalms 127:3 AMP

To my baby boy

My little one.

You are enough.

Cry if you need to.

I hear you. .

I see you.

I will protect you.

Children are God's love-gift from the Lord, The
fruit of the womb a reward.

Psalms 127:3 TPT

Love-Kingdom Vibes Only

Xiomara

To my warrior princess,
I don't know all the battles you will fight
But it is my life's mission
That you will not fight the battles
    I am fighting today.
I have committed myself to doing the work now.
Not so that you will live a soft life,
But your own life;
Paving your own way
I wish for you not to fight the
    battles of your ancestors,
Because we conquered those villains today.
My warrior princess,
Xiomara
I charge you
Put on the full armor of God
To forge ahead and clear the path
    for the ones to come.
Fight the good fight of faith,
But you will never fight alone.
We love you!
We are proud of you! There is much more
    on the other side of this war!
Know and embrace who you are
So that the war that you fight will not be within.
Know whose you are,

So you can identify your opponent.

Be still.

Study his tactics.

For he is studying you.

The battle is not what you see before you.

Be still.

Listen to the Commander

My warrior princess.

You are here, for such a time as this.

It is time for you to carry on the mantle,

Remember you are never alone.

The God of Angel Armies is with you.

Be still.

Listen for his instructions.

Be battle ready.

Shine-Most beautiful one.

The victory is yours.

Train up a child in the way he should go [teaching him to seek God's wisdom and will for his abilities and talents], Even when he is old he will not depart from it.

Proverbs 22:6 AMP

Kai

As living water

You will bring healing to the souls around you.

You will be abundant,

Abundant in joy, peace, and power.

The enemy will be no match for

    you, young warrior.

Out of your belly shall flow rivers of water.

The Spirit of God is in you.

Be still and listen

To the voice of your Commander.

You will bring order to chaos

Because the King is in you.

Your words will be seasoned with peace.

Your words will give life.

So be careful what you say.

Your strength comes from your obedience

You are as vast and magnanimous as the sea.

But you must obey the limitations of

    the shore set in place by God.

Obedience is the key to your victory.

Great warrior prince,

Put on the full armor of God.

Every place you set your foot God will give you

When you give God your life in surrender.

Let him authorize every decision.

Listen for his approval.

Pay attention to God's traffic signs, stop, wait, go.

Nothing is impossible for God.

Remember you will never fight alone.

Protect the marginalized.

Love the unlovable.

Remember the forgotten.

Your presence is a gift to us.

We love you.

We are proud of you.

Go and make disciples.

Make God proud.

Dedicate your child to God and point them in the
way that they should go, and the values they've
learned from you will be with them for life.

Proverbs 22:6 TPT

Love-Kingdom Vibes Only

Meditation #5

One of the practices we see often in the Old Testament is the patriarch, very close to his death, giving a special blessing to the future generation. I think though it may have been a sad time everyone looked forward to what would be the pronouncement over the lives of the next generation. It was basically the last will and testament, but also well wishes came with it. Is there a generational blessing for us? What is our inheritance?

Romans 8:17 TPT says, "And since we are his true children, we qualify to share all his treasures, for indeed, we are heirs of God himself. And since we are joined to Christ, we also inherit all that he is and all that he has. We will experience being co-glorified with him provided that we accept his suffering as our own."

It is comforting to know that our inheritance is not tied to us and our ability to do right. But it is tied to Jesus and his righteousness, and he has already overcome sin. Imagine all that has been allocated to Jesus also being set aside for you and me. My mind can barely conceive it. But all will soon dim in comparison to the Lord. He is our greatest treasure.

Read:

· Romans 8

Exnihilo

Exnihilo
To build a family out of nothing
No blueprint
Yes, I'm an architect.
With no daddy to pass down the design
But you want me to lay down the foundation.
Buried beneath the disappointments
The empty seat in the stands
Mommy's overnight shifts
Then she shifted gears to tears
My trips to Sears
Looking for the materials
To make this house a home.
But you say you don't need a man
You got your own.
So tell me, where do I fit in?

I'm rehearsing a script from my own improv
Because my Pops was a touring actor.
You seem to have it all together.
Tell me, who is your director?

You're rehearsing the lines from
    your mom's screenplay, "The Diary
    of a Mad Black Woman"
You take center stage,
Your actions screaming verbatim
"I can do bad all by myself"

Exnihilo
Both standing here "Waiting to Exhale"
Not sure what the next act should be
Because Disney never showed us
What happened after the "Happily Ever After"

Looking at the castle
Knowing there has to be better than this
But..
What will we see on our closing credits?
How do we get from nothing to something?
From fatherless to "Daddy's home"
From latchkey kid to "Come down for dinner."
From "I don't need a man" to "I have need of you."

I learned how to be ready for battle,
But never knew how to lay down my weapons.
Be patient with me.
I'm working on this,
Exnihilo.

"Be imitators of God in everything you do, for
then you will represent your Father as his be-
loved sons and daughters. And continue to walk
surrendered to the extravagant love of Christ,
for he surrendered his life as a sacrifice for us.
His great love for us was pleasing to God, like
an aroma of adoration—a sweet healing fra-
grance."

Ephesians 5:1-2 TPT

Joseph, did you know?

Joseph, Did you know?
Mary was blessed among women
   not only because she carried the
   savior but because she had you
Joseph a man of principle
You became her bodyguard when the
   assault of insecurities and doubts were
   destined to be hurled at her like stones
Unexpectedly you were fast forwarded
   into a role of Redeemer
You understood the assignment and you
   painstakingly made preparations and
   took the long journey towards healing
You sojourned with Mary through the
   dark cold nights of despair
But you covered her in prayer
Like the High Priest in the order of Melchizedek
You sacrificed your pride on the altar
And daily you picked up her cross
Joseph did you know?
That you would be the purpose partner of a
   woman whose baby would change the world
You were faithful in little things
Diligently searching for shelter
Trading places

You became the midwife
Safely transporting the celestial
    to the terrestrial
You performed a miracle
Your husbandry made a flower bloom
The girl who was once rejected and despised
Now venerated as blessed among women
Joseph did you know
What the warmth of your eyes could do?
Your eyes crowned her and
    made her your queen
She gave birth to the Prince of Peace
At once all the pain seemed to cease
Joseph did you know?
Your hands would train a boy to be a King
The same hands that carved wood
Cradled the face of the Messiah
Joseph did you know that your unfailing
    love changed world history?
When everyone else wanted to choose violence
You chose love
You adopted Love
They called him, Jesus

When Joseph woke up from his dream, he did all
that the angel of the Lord instructed him to do.
He took Mary to be his wife,

Matthew 1:24 TPT

Meditation #6

I believe one of the biggest markers of the presence of God is unity. Conversely, if there is anything the devil hates it's unity. He has been attacking it since his "coup-de-etat" in heaven then he continued it here on earth with the first family.

Unity was one of the main things Jesus prayed for in what is referred to as his "High Priestly Prayer" in John 17:11 TPT. It says, "...Holy Father, each one that you have given me, keep them in your name so that they will be united as one, even as we are one."

If we look at the unity present in the church of Acts, we see that it created the perfect atmosphere for all the other "fruits" of the spirit.The presence of God made the impossible possible. I would encourage you to invite God into your daily situations, especially your family life.

There was no lack where the presence of God was. There was an abundance of generosity amongst the members. There was an undying commitment to service to God and others. There was boldness for the sake of the gospel.

Often times as Christians, we compartmentalize this spiritual phenomenon to what God can and will do for the church, forsaking the ministry of the home which God gave us as our first responsibility. The enemy takes advantage of our ignorance and lack of diligence in this department. Our stewardship of our families or lack thereof impacts the communities we are a part of and eventually eternity.

It is our duty to take an active role in cultivating a rich atmosphere for our families to grow and thrive in light of eternity. Every day on this side of eternity is an investment in the one to come.

Read:

- John 17:11
- Acts 4:32

Prayer Challenge #6:

- Pray for your (future) children or children around you, that they will grow in wisdom, stature and favor with God and man.
- Ask God to help you to be a good role model for the children around you
- Ask God to help you to understand the uniqueness of your (future) child and how to best parent them
- Ask God to help you guide and advise your children or children around you according to God's word with love

Do:

- Volunteer at a foster home or anywhere with children
- Spend time with a child
- Tell your child about their birth story
- Think about your best childhood memory

Journal:

- What did the younger you need to hear growing up?
- As a spouse what could you do better to be a better influence for your spouse?
- How could you be a better role model?
- What habits could you start doing to promote a better holistic life? Pray about it.

Kingdom Community

Love-Kingdom Vibes Only

In the Kingdom: There is
diversity, and empathy.

The Kingdom

The Kingdom is not some unreachable utopic place or experience

It's His palpable presence

The Eden restored

The sacred place

Elevated above what man can see and tarnish

Built and established to be perfected and pro-tected within you

No longer will time nor space drive a wedge between the greatest lover of your soul

Because the King has raised up his Kingdom on the foundation of your heart

The kingdom is not discovered in one place or another, for God's kingdom realm is already expanding with some of you.

Luke 17:21 TPT

Love-Kingdom Vibes Only

Golden History

In their miseducation of us
They would have you believe our story
   is all dark, cursed, and black
Like our sun kissed hue
Our history is golden
Our history's streets are paved
   in precious stones
In a drop step to the rhythmic beat
   of our talking drums
Our ancestors left their brilliance along the way

They came trying to steal our shine
They came trying to steal our thunder
They came trying to silence our voices
They came telling us we didn't
   know our own God

They made our history black
Black with grief, pain, anger, and nostalgia
But we remembered

The golden dust of our land
Oh how the Sun smiled on us
Oh how the Son smiled on us
We birthed freedom writers
   and freedom fighters
Who told you our history was black?

Baby, we are golden!
From royalty, you were chosen!
Sing,Dance, Write, Run, Play, Act, Love
We have overcome!

What they meant for evil
Nyame (God)- meant for good...
Who told you our history was black?

Yes, we have been through fire
Through the scourge of institutionalized
    oppression from generation to generation
Look at our skin
We are now pure Gold.

By God's grace, though it hurt,
    we are still thriving
Awurade, Meda wo ase
That is, God I thank you
Our history only becomes golden and our
    future becomes as brilliant as a diamond
When we remember our God.

I have watched and seen how my people have
been mistreated in Egypt. I have heard their
painful groaning, and now I have come down to
set them free...

Acts 7:34 TPT

A Safe Church

I, too, like the watchman, look for that day

The anxious, ruminating mind

    would enter those doors

And leave with a sound mind

I, too, wait for the day

The naked man would enter those doors

And leave fully clothed and with

    a bed prepared for him

I, too, pray for that day

The sin sick soul

Would find people who care enough

To lend a listening ear

To confess to

And throw him on the backs of their prayers

And embrace him with the Father's love

I,too, yearn for the day
That lack would be eradicated
Because what's mine is yours
"Mi casa es su casa"
My love is your love
My God is your God

I, too, earnestly hope for the day
That there will be no need for doors
Because church will no longer be
    isolated to the four walls
But we would be so intermingled seamlessly in
    the community where we are planted that
When you see the community
You see Church
When the community sees the Church
The community sees
God

I, bless the day
That our community
Will see God.

A deep sense of holy awe swept over everyone,
and the apostles performed many miraculous
signs and wonders. All the believers were in
fellowships as one body,and they shared with
one another whatever they had.

Acts 2:43–44 TPT

Love-Kingdom Vibes Only

Meditation #7

Often times people look at diversity as a bad thing but in many ways, it was encouraged by God. In Genesis 11:4, where we find the story of Tower of Babel, he had instructed the people to disperse over the entire face of the earth. Though they shared a language he didn't make them to be in one place. They used the one thing they had in common to not make God's name great, but their own. The Lord said that when we lift his name up, he will draw all man unto him, but look at what happens when we do the opposite? When we lift ourselves up, especially as a community, we lose sight of our need for God and exalt our own capabilities. This is pride. God comes down and decides to remove the thing that unified them, their language, because they would continue to be disobedient.

Let's look at what happens when God unifies a group of people. The scripture says in Acts 2, that as the people were gathered to celebrate Pentecost (Feast of Weeks), which was a time of returning a portion of their harvest back to God among other festivals. As they were celebrating these festivals in obedience, they happened to be in one place, but people had traveled far and wide "from every nation under heaven" to be able to celebrate the feasts in Jerusalem. The Spirit of the Lord descended on them in that place and people were given the ability to speak out "clearly and appropriately" in diverse languages.

I can truly appreciate this as a miracle as a person who dedicated more than ten years of my life to studying Spanish and learning other languages along the way. It is a long process to reach fluency in a language. But the Spirit in a moment, caused them to be able to speak so that men from different parts of the world understood clearly as if having a simultaneous interpreter present! The same mechanism that was confusion in the past, the Lord utilized to bring himself glory, because those who were present were obedient. God can do remarkable things with our unity, but only when it is subject to his will. Unity in our hands becomes self-seeking. If you continue to read this story, you will see that through the work of the Holy Spirit the new Christian community sounds almost utopic. The unity of that community was characterized by self-sacrificing; hospitality and spiritual breakthroughs were able to occur freely. I wonder how many things the Lord has not been able to do in our communities, because we let frivolous things divide us.

Read:

- Genesis 11
- Acts 2

Breathe

A collective gasp rang out as
   you expelled your last.
As your life was being expunged you bid
   farewell to your life giver, "mama."
As a child screaming for justice
   in a sibling fight "Mama!"
27 I can't breathes fell on dead hearts.
As you have always done, you bared
   the weight of the oppressor on
   your neck risking paralysis.
We beckon Mama justice! Because
   Daddy law has gone rogue.
With our last breath we will call to order
   those who are out of order for those
   who wear the fatigue and suffer .
For them this revolution will be televised
   until the proverbial sepulcher
   of racism is off our backs;

Until our lifeless bodies are no longer a threat.
Celebrate with those who celebrate, and weep
with those who grieve. Live happily together in a
spirit of harmony, and be as mindful of another's
worth as you are your own..."

Romans 12:15-16 TPT

Sound the alarm

I cried today
Because instead of coloring my
    drawing with sky blue
It was code blue get under the desks
    there's an active shooter.
My red crayon fell to the ground
Like the teacher from across the hall
Today the bell
Didn't release us for lunch
It just made us more aware of how
    time wasn't in our hands but the
    hand of the one with the gun.
I cried today not while saying
    goodbye to mom and dad,
But because the bell went off one last
    time and just like every other day it
    cut our time short but this time
I won't ever say goodbye to mom and dad
    again.I hope this time the alarm would
    be loud enough to wake everyone up.
To draw another picture,
One where schools and churches really
    were safe sanctuaries again.
Where everyone took their shoes off,
    checked their motives at the threshold in
    reverence of who were inside ...humanity.
The place in which God resides.
Would they still dare to touch the anointed?
The kingdom lives in each of us
Act accordingly.

He will wipe away every tear from their eyes
and eliminate death entirely. No one will mourn
or will or weep any longer. The pain of wounds
will no longer exist, for the old order has
ceased."

Revelation 21:4 TPT

Dar a luz

Let there be light

Life is light

Giving birth is bringing that which

  was composed in the dark into

  the limelight of center stage

The phenomenon of giving light

Giving birth

Is quickly transformed into giving darkness

When black mothers lay vulnerably

On the mercy tables

Of merciless

Non-colored practitioners

Who flip the script and flip the switch

Let there be Darkness

This little light of ours

They won't let us shine

So the king of Egypt called for the midwives
and said to them, "Why have you done this thing,
and allowed the boy babies to live?...And be-
cause the midwives feared God [with profound
reverence], He established families and house-
holds for them.

Exodus 1:18,21 AMP

Love Kingdom Vibes Only

The real pursuit of love is finding

   God in every relationship

He made us in his image

So we should reflect love

God is love

So finding him is finding love

So I guess love shouldn't be so hard to find, right?

The one who doesn't love has yet to know God,
for God is love.

1 John 4:8 TPT

Fall together

Since the first fall in Genesis

We've been falling like leaves in Autumn

But the one time He rose, saved us for eternity

As the leaves transform

So does he change our circumstances

    around for our good

But in the same way they grow morbid

    separated from the tree

So do we as we're separated from the Vine

I am the sprouting vine and you're my branch-
es. As you live in union with me as your source
fruitfulness will stream from within you – but
when you live separated from me you are pow-
erless.

John 15:5 TPT

Prayer Challenge #7

Ask God to help you to be the hands and feet of God to make a change.

Ask the Lord for wisdom/discipline to do what is right in his eyes

Ask the Lord for the presence of the Holy Spirit in your home and to transform the heart of your family to be one of selflessness, unity, and love.

Ask the Lord to grant you discernment, so that you can identify safe people and safe environments

Ask the Lord to teach you how to trust again

Do:

- Find an organization that is working towards the effort you are passionate about.
- Donate or volunteer.
- Bring awareness to the issue.

Ponder/Journal:

- What societal issue upsets you most?
- What community/groups do you feel most accepted in? Why?
- What community/groups do you feel most rejected in? Why?

Love-Kingdom Vibes Only

CONVOS WITH
THE KING

Love-Kingdom Vibes Only

In the Kingdom:There is identity, comfort, and true love.

Name change

Thank you for changing my name

From Marah to Naomi

From bitter to sweetness

From pain to favor

From abandoned to chosen

For the one who is victorious, I will make you to be a pillar in the sanctuary of my God, permanently sure. I will write on you the name of my God-the New Jerusalem, descending from my God out of heaven. And I'll write my own name on you.

Revelation 3:12 TPT

Prayer Challenge #8

Ask God to help you to reflect his character

Ask God to rewrite your story to align with the destiny he has for you

Do:

Read/Pray these scriptures back to God:

- 1 John 3:2
- Isaiah 61:1
- Romans 1:7
- Hebrews 13:5
- Romans 6:6
- Romans 8:16
- Ephesians 1:6
- Ephesians 1:4
- Ephesians 2:10

Can I get a refill?

With the heat of the sun blazing
Everyone is starting to look the same.
With the screech of the crows in my head
Circling around my dead hopes and dreams
Everyone sounds the same.
Sending in their request to fulfill their desires
Like a DJ
I'm mixing and matching
Flipping and spinning
To the rhythms of my masters.

"Give me a drink "
Another request at the bar of probably
Another man who sees me as
    just a Coca Cola bottle
Sprite
Just to quench his thirst
Who cares that I've been walking these
    desert streets for 29 years
Searching for my own bartender
Shelves out of stock
But the bell keeps ringing.

"Give me a drink "
Another empty handed man
For me to fill, build, and thrill
My eyes never met the stranger
But something about him felt familiar
Tired of being the benefactor to my own demise
I asked, " Where is your cup? What do you have
    to offer me? What do you bring to the table?"

For years I have poured from my broken
    cistern? Laboring to maintain enough
    droplets in the gourd for me.
But by the time, I draw the cracked pot to
    my lips the last drop hydrates the floor
Cursed with a broken pot.
I have had 5 broken pots.
Broken heart
Broken trust
Broken belief
Broken home
Broken body

This last pot, religion.
Stolen and dirty

The pot of my ancestors
They told me that this pot only works
    when it is used in rituals
So I have dunked it sanctimoniously
Chanted empty words
Void of love and grace
Shoved it beneath the water in despair
Trying to wash away all my shame

Pushed the stone away on my own
So that may be God would notice my hard work
Came to the well alone
To show my definition of dedication
My pot it only serves one, me
If I worship this way, maybe you would hear me
If I gave, you would give to me

Now you ask me to give you a drink
But I have a broken pot.
I had five pots before.
Now I have nothing to draw with.

I served other gods:

God of trauma
God of lust
God of unforgiveness
God of fear
God of pride

They became my masters.
Why would you a King want a slave girl like me?
He replied, "When you served these
    other gods, you gave everything."

"That is where I want to be. Surrounded by
your everything. Nothing satisfies me except
you. Water is essential and so are you to me.
I want to be essential for you too. I am the
gift that keeps on giving. I don't take what I
can't restore. Your previous masters stole,
killed, and destroyed. I came to give you life.

This pot you carry, religion will not fill you.
I came to give you me, which is greater
than this pot. It can't contain me. Let
me fill you. Let me make room. I don't
come to make withdrawals where I don't
deposit. You have been trying to earn my
love, but I want to put my love in you. It
will flow from you like rivers. It will heal
your wounds and those around you."

The cracked pot fell from my hands
Breaking my contracts with my slave masters
He said, "I Am"
He is the one..
The mender of broken hearts
The greatest lover of my soul
The one who loved the unlovable
Forgave the unforgivable
Gave sight to the pain-stricken eyes
Released me from the enemy's grip

So I quickly sent out my wedding invitations
Come see the man
Who saw my faults
And loved me still
The man who deposited love into
   a bankrupt account
And said I was enough
This is a love worth dying for.
This is a love worth living for.

Jesus said to her, "You don't have to wait any
longer, the Anointed One is here speaking with
you–I am the One you're looking for.

John 4:26 TPT

Meditation #8

Full transparency, the poem "Can I get a refill?" came at a time where I felt like God was asking for too much. I felt justified. I felt wronged and wanted vengeance. I felt up until this point, I had done church and Christianity and all the things, checking all the boxes. But he asked me to forgive the people I thought did the unforgivable to me. It felt unfair for me to be the one who was wronged to be asked to forgive.

Needless to say, I was about to give up on religion. That was exactly what needed to go. I found myself not trusting God and having a banter with him similar to the woman at the well. I had eloquent theology, but my heart was empty. I couldn't check forgiveness off my "to do" list so I wanted to quit God. That's religion, but God was calling me higher. It was a similar conversation as he had with the rich young ruler. He was only missing one thing, which Jesus himself said. Often times we hold on to things even things like pride and unforgiveness not realizing that it is that very thing that is hindering our relationship with Christ.

Many of you know the story of the rich young ruler, he cherished his life as it was and his sense of righteousness on his terms so much so that he was willing to walk away from his opportunity of walking with Jesus for the rest of his life. I guess the only question left to be asked is what are you holding on to more than Jesus? Is it worth eternity?

Read:

- Matthew 19:20–30
- John 4:5–30

Love-Kingdom Vibes Only

God over Mind

That test was a part of my testimony

Took a stroll through Death's Valley

It was just a destination.

It will not be my destiny.

It will not be my children's portion.

I will take my thoughts captive

Locking them away with the keys of Truth.

His promises will comfort me like Tempurpedic

Because I will make a mansion

    for him in my mind,

Soft life

The scarlet letter of shame

Is no match for the scarlet blood of the Lamb

There is grace for the afflicted

Get up

He has made me whole

Fill your thoughts with my words until they pen-
etrate deep into your spirit.

Proverbs 4:21 TPT

Sundays

A day of darkness and enlightenment
The sun's rays can leave you in a daze
Days like these sheds light on the
    need for an embrace
Sundays seem to stand still
Long enough to catch your breath and
    short enough to suffocate.
Sun days yet cloudy with thoughts
    and fleeting emotions.
How can they become Son days?
Days when I gaze in your face to see your heart
Days when I'm reminded of the great
    affection and care you have towards me
Son days, days of rest and gladness
Daze of hope
Days where you remind me that I
    am yours and you are mine.
What will it take for everyday to be a Son day?
One where I remember that I am
    no longer an orphan.
That the sub-zero temps of sin
    no longer has my heart.
Oh to be engulfed by you.
Sundays

Why are you in despair, O my soul? And why
are you restless and disturbed within me? Hope
in God and wait expectantly for Him, for I shall
again praise Him, The help of my [sad] counte-
nance and my God.

Psalms 43:5 AMP

Love-Kingdom Vibes Only

Jehovah El Roi

Abandonment taught you...

 that God hears the unheard and sees the unseen,

he was always there.

 It taught you ...

never to overlook the unseen or unheard

Then she called the name of the Lord who spoke to her, "You are God Who Sees"; for she said, "Have I not even here [in the wilderness] remained alive after seeing Him [who sees me with understanding and compassion]?

Genesis 16:13 AMP

God's love

Real love isn't earned.

God's love is a gift

Accept it.

We have come into an intimate experience with God's love, and we trust in the love he has for us. God is love! Those who are living in love are living in God, and God lives through them.

1 John 4:16 TPT

Coupon

You showed me a love

I couldn't afford to pay

Then you gave me the receipt

Stamped

Paid In full

He himself will redeem you; he will ransom you
from the cruel slavery of your sins!

Psalms 130:8 TPT

My Original Trinity

Woman at the Well

Hagar

Leah

Woman at the Well

Looking for love in dry places

Isolated myself from intimacy

S on my chest

For Shame not Strength

Chose the brightest time of the day

Because it is actually easier to hide in plain sight

Until God showed me himself...

Hagar

In a strange land

From my home land

New way of living

New way of loving

Only had a piece of him

And a part of a promise

Guess it's better than nothing

But treated like nothing

With a responsibility bigger than me

Better to die in the desert

Than to suffer in plenty

Until God came running after me...

Leah

Not beautiful enough to catch
    your eye on your IG feed
But you used my body as your amusement park
Going through the labor of producing
Any and everything
I thought would make me number 1
Until I realized..
I was always God's number 1.

Like the woman at the well,
I am filled with the living,
healing waters of the Holy Spirit
Like Hagar,
His love, goodness, and mercy pursue me,
Like Leah,
Man may not have seen me as ideal
But I was always God's number 1 draft pick.

But you are God's chosen treasure- priests who
are kings, a spiritual "nation" set apart as God's
devoted ones. He called you out of darkness
to experience his marvelous light, and now he
claims you as his very own. He did this so that
you would broadcast his glorious wonders
throughout the world.

1 Peter 2:9 TPT

Idol

Dear Abba,

Help me never to make him my god

But to see God in him

For only a fool would trade the unfading splen-
dor of the immortal God to worship the fading
image of other humans, idols made to look like
people, animals, birds, and even creeping rep-
tiles!

Romans 1:23 TPT

Love-Kingdom Vibes Only

The Choice

Thanks for making the decision

To love me at the most painful

    moment of your life

I know you loved me before the

    Earth was formed

But there's something about how you chose me

    in the midst of your agony in Gethsemane

It's amazing how you thought I was worth it

There's something about how you chose me in

    the lowest time of your life that hits different

Anyone can say they love me when

    they're in a good mood

But you did it while you were feeling rejected,

    betrayed, abandoned and in pain.

Help me to choose to love you even in

    the crushing moments of life.

Even though I am torn within, and my soul is in turmoil, I will not ask the Father to rescue me from this hour of trial. For I have come to fulfill my purpose- to offer myself to God.

John 12:27 TPT

Meditation #9

The most mind-blowing and confusing thing about creation was not the fact that mosquitos or roaches were created but that the freedom of choice was established. Through the annals of time, since the fall we see God persistently choosing people who refuse/unable to choose him.

When Jesus was in Gethsemane, this was where we really got an up-close look at what it takes to love us. He had to pray multiple times for strength. It got him to the cross, but on the cross he saw a side of the Father that he never knew, his back. He chose to stick to the mission, so that we could always enjoy the invitation to be with Abba face to face.

In order for us to embrace Abba's love, we also have to embrace Jesus' suffering. It was Jesus' choice to suffer that gives us this new life. We can't enjoy the fruit without taking part in the process that brought it to life. Jesus promised us that we would never have to go through this life and its difficulties alone, because he left us the Comforter/Helper. So, we can make the choice for him without fear because his Comforter/Helper is with us and will see us through all we face.

Prayer Challenge #9

- Ask God to help you to choose to live for him daily
- Ask God to help you to surrender your will for his
- Ask God to help you to have an experiential knowledge of him

Read:

- Matthew 26:36–46
- Read Philippians 3:10

Lover

Lover of my soul
You've taken painstaking time to know me
Endured pain to love me
You've sketched out time from
   now til eternity to heal me

My Lover
My Ever present God showers
   me in undivided attention
Wraps me in arms of grace
Clothes me with his mercy
Kisses me with kindness
What manner of love is this?

When from my abuser I ran
You ran towards me
When battered and defaced by guilt and shame
You saw me
You see me as a bride awaiting her groom
What manner of love is this?

When my body went limp

Too bruised to be held

Tears like runaway slaves

Your words of truth soothed

    my internal bleeding

Your promises became my bandages

Oh lover of my soul, how could I repay?

One day with pain in his eyes

He clothed himself not in armor

But in my guilt and shame

I asked him, why?

He placed my puzzled face in his hands

"You were created to be loved"

"The greatest love I can show you, is to

    abandon the comfort of my throne"

"Experience your hurt"

"The greatest gift I have for you is

    eternal quality time with me

What kind of lover would I be if I was

    only with you in the good times?

I've seen your pain and I have heard your cry
I am going to set the wrong right."
He said , "I do this so you will see and believe
    that you will never fight alone."

"Your abuser wants what he can't have."
"He can't have your love for me."
"He can't have your heart."
"He can't have your commitment."
"He can't have my power."
"He can't have me."
"The me I placed inside of you."

"Lay all your cares on me for I care
    for you," he continued.
"My burden is light, let me handle it all."
"I've never lost a fight."
"Let me fight this one."
I bowed my head,
"My groom, for whom I have long
    awaited. Take your rightful place and
    let the enemies be scattered."

Yahweh, you are my soul's celebration. How
could I ever forget the miracles of kindness
you've done for me?

Psalms 103:2 TPT

Love~Kingdom Vibes Only

Meditation #10

One of my favorite attributes of God is illustrated best in the story of Hagar. She had such a personal yet not so glamorous history with God. Yet, she had the privilege of naming God due to her circumstance and in those times the only one really naming anyone was a man. Without justifying whether she was wrong or right, she was in a situation where she was not being treated well and had to run away. In the middle of nowhere in what seemed like a hopeless situation God pursued her and called her by name. She was so shocked, she said this is a "God who sees me." She named him "Jehovah El-Roi."

There is another situation I want to bring your attention to which is found in Song of Songs. The Shulamite woman/ The bride is separated from her Beloved and she goes out to find him but she's beaten by those who are in charge of guarding the city. Song of Songs 5:6-7

In both these situations people who were to be trusted with their wellbeing mistreated these women in some way. This is the story of many in our world today, both men and women.

I was comforted in the story of Hagar to know that God pursued her and made himself known to her a slave girl, who the society thought was insignificant, so much so he allowed her to give him a name, which is so intimate and gives her value. I want to let you know that God sees, hears and cares. The story goes on to say that he blessed her son, which is a generational blessing. This means he still remembers Hagar and he will never forget you.

Prayer Challenge #10

In what ways have you been mistreated by people you trusted?

 Ask God to help you to heal from those wounds and help you to release the pain and the people to him.

What situations do you want God to remember on your behalf?

What blessing do you want God to give not only you but your future generations?

Do:

Read Genesis 16

Read Song of Songs 5

Introvert

I love that you were just like me
   when you were here
You spent a lot of time alone and in prayer
You had a small friend circle
Though you were empathetic to everyone
You were balanced
You went to weddings (I love those)
I like how you observed people
You were active in church but you took
   church outside, you traveled !
You loved deep convos and intimacy
I appreciate you for making it ok to be me
As I'm learning more about introversion
   I see that you lived a powerful life
   even when you had to slip away
I loved that you cared about those you
   were with and you care about me
Thank you for loving me and creating me as I am
Show me how to love me too

Early in the morning, while it was still dark,
Jesus got up, left [the house], and went out to a
scheduled place, and was praying there.

Mark 1:35 AMP

Grace

I love you

I know my capacity to love you is far inferior

to your expression of love for me but as the

woman who washed your feet with her tears

Please accept my gratitude for your grace

I thank you for the distance you traveled to

rescue me from the cross and instead

you surrendered your life for mine

I hate that I can't pay you back

I Know there's nothing I could do

to even earn your love

Though I do try

I wanna show you that it was all worth it

I'm so used to working so hard for everything

I have even the affection of those in my life

But you're different

And it should be a relief but it feels

    uncomfortable and makes me anxious

Help me to love you back the way you deserve

I just wanna make you proud

I know my actions should've forfeited your love

    even before I was born but for your grace

I have no one as loyal to me as you

Who else can I trust?

If not for your grace where and who would I be?

I'm tempted to ask, Why me?

"Who am I that you're mindful of me?"

I thank you ABBA

Show me how to love you back.

Your grace is confusing, but I wouldn't

    have it any other way

For it is by grace [God's remarkable compassion and favor drawing you to Christ] that you have been saved [actually delivered from judgment and given eternal life] through faith. And this [salvation] is not of yourselves [not through your own effort], but it is the [undeserved, gracious] gift of God;

Ephesians 2:8 AMP

Meditation #11

Then suddenly the voice of the Father shouted from the sky, saying, "This is my Son—the Beloved! My greatest delight is in him!

Matthew 3:17

This scripture became very near and dear to my heart when I noticed the timeline of events. We live in a very performance driven society. We live for likes, applauses and follows. One doesn't get a bonus until he has gotten the big contract. However, Jesus got the greatest endorsement one could ever get, before he ever lifted a finger or healed the first sick person.

What does that say about you and I? It says that we don't earn God's affection. It is reminiscent to the love at first sight that parents have for their children, there is nothing the child did to earn that love but to exist. The poem "Grace" illustrates the "tug of war" we all feel well when we come face to face with God's love. We want to pay back but we feel a level of angst when we find that what we have to offer doesn't seem to measure up. It's overwhelming. But our job is to accept the free gift and out of our gratitude we will live to please the one who will become our delight.

Prayer Challenge #11

Ask God to reveal and remove anything that is an obstacle to the intimacy he wants to have with you.

Ask God to help you experience the Father's love and to reveal your identity in him.

Ask God to help you to make him your delight

Do:

- Read Romans 8
- Read Hosea

Provider

I have to admit I can't be my own provider
My resources often run out
Just like my patience and strength
Your word reminded me that you are
    willing to give me a break from my
    every day burdens...even when I think I
    should be strong enough to carry it

Sometimes we get stuck on the
    resources you can provide and not
    the rest we so desperately need

Today "Jehovah Jireh" means
    something a little different
Sometimes my greatest need is not the
    resource but the reset you provide

Thank you Abba,

With love,
Your child

So there remains a [full and complete] Sabbath
rest for the people of God.

Hebrews 4:9 TPT

Prayer Challenge #12

"Are you weary, carrying a heavy burden? Come to me. I will refresh your life, for I am your oasis."

Matthew 11:28 TPT

What burdens do you need God to carry for you?

What parts of your life feel like a desert and needs a refreshing of his love, anointing, reassurance, direction?

Take a moment and pray/journal whatever comes to mind.

Ask God for wisdom in an area you feel you are lacking

Love-Kingdom Vibes Only

Works Cited

Adu, Sade. "Cherish the Day." *Youtube*.https://www.youtube.com/watch?v=Y7JuCab6yqs&ab_channel=Sade-Topic

Chapman, Gary D. The Five Love Languages. Walker Large Print, 2010.

Diary of a Mad Black Woman. Directed by Darren Grant. Lionsgate Films,2005.

Fentress, Valerie, et al. "Myrrh Definition and Meaning – Bible Dictionary." biblestudytools.com, www.biblestudytools.com/dictionary/myrrh. Accessed 30 Oct. 2022.

Flowers, Jerry. "#Kingdomvibesonly." *YouTube*, www.youtube.com/playlist?list=PL5WSu5tEDyGaGCFYL9wDF-U2w2lIRPIjC. Accessed 25 Oct. 2021.

Neyo. "Never Knew I Needed." *Youtube*. https://www.youtube.com/watch?v=iKKdJr42wOY&ab_channel=DisneyMusicVEVO.

The Holy Bible: The Amplified Bible. 1987. 2015. La Habra, CA: The Lockman Foundation.

Thomas, Gary. The Sacred Search: Updated and Revised. Revised, David C Cook, 2021.

Waiting to Exhale. Directed by Forest Whitaker.20th Century Fox,1995.

Other Publications

Poetry Collections on Amazon:

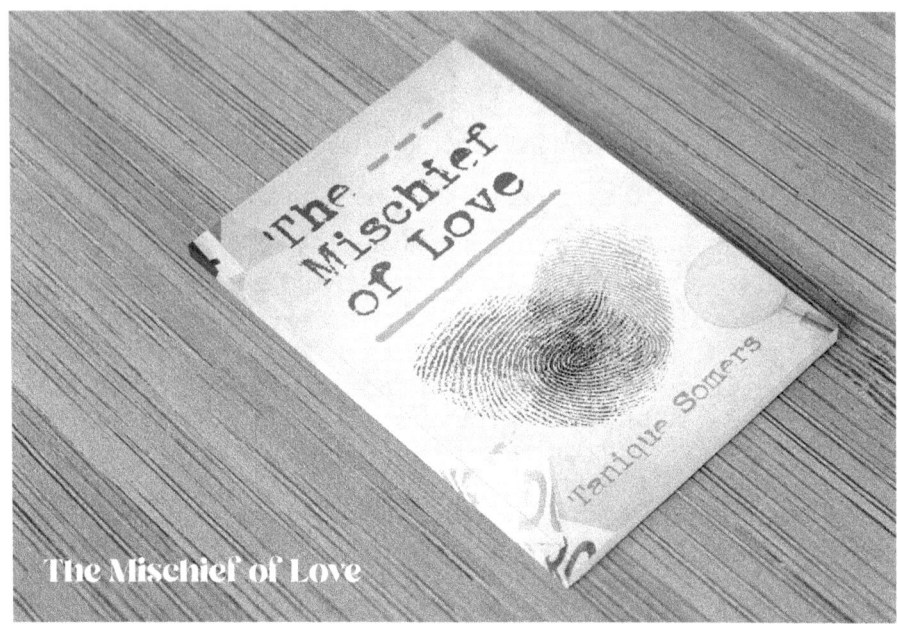

The Mischief of Love

La Travesura de Amor